Suicide Is A Serious Killer

Let's End It Today

Written by

Evadynè Smith

©January 2018

ISBN-13:978-1983667237
ISBN-10:1983667234

Dedication

This book is dedicated to my daughter and grandson, may this seed never enter or grow in your lives. Here's to your happiness forever. Love you both, as much as you feel and know.

To my parents, Smitty and Peola; For if you did not feed me, clothe me, believe in me, provide me with your intellect and spirituality, never doubt me, (just admitting, confused by some of my decisions), play the music that I listened carefully to, take me to dance class, tell me to "stop playing so much", and that, "everything is not a game", make the decisions that you made so that we could live where we lived, grant me to be the middle born child of the 8, living siblings, who grew up together, which I believe was also a research platform for my understanding of people the way I do; lots of practice in "observation of personalities" you know, love and understand you all, my siblings; if it were not for the both of you, my Parents, I would not be the person that I am today. If those things did not happen, I would not have continued on to meet and interact with the many people that I have throughout my life, from family to friends to neighbors to teachers to shoppers in the grocery store, all of whom have had an influence on my life in some way.

A very special thank you and much love to my Uncle Leroy, for his continued support, wisdom talks, understanding of me and for being the Patriarch of my family. To my Aunt Hurley, who knows me well and realizes my true being, love you and thank you for all that you have done for the family. To my sister Renee for her enduring patience, encouragement of my skills and tolerance of my deadlines, I love and thank you endlessly. To Gail, for the talks of shared memories, special recognition of who I am, from the start, inside and out and for reminding me to dedicate this book, I love and thank you.

I am ever so grateful for my relationship with the Creator, allowing me to stay awake, stay prepared, remain in pay attention mode and for the ability to communicate well enough to share all that I am guided to share.

Grateful too, that the University of the Universe is tuition free, open 24/7 earth time, and that I am accepted as a lifetime student.
For all of the above, I am thankful.

Lastly, and most importantly, I dedicate this book to all of the lives it will change and save!

2

Preface

**Contact the National Suicide Prevention Lifeline
1–800–273-TALK (8255)
The deaf and hard of hearing can contact the
Lifeline via TTY at 1-800-799-4889**

Demystifying suicide and identifying some of what causes it will help put a stop to this killer.

Feeling sad and lonely...with no hope in sight...that's what most people feel about the victims of this killer, called suicide. Loved ones can only guess what was going on in the persons mind and life at the time they decided to end it.

Some victims of this killer gave it much thought and attention. They took the time to create the plan of when and how. Some wrote notes or made a call and of course some did none of the above. Well the act of letting this killer win required thinking and finally a decision in itself.

Then in some cases it was a quick thought, then action, with no pre-existing conditions of emotional distress, sadness or feeling hopeless, in fact it was simply the side effect of sourced medications or drugs. The reality of this effect is more common than we know, and many people aren't thinking about it at all. We hear the commercial warnings, "may cause suicidal thoughts", but we never think about what those thoughts would sound like.

Let us see how we can change some of this. What can we do to better arm ourselves and others against its attack? Let's begin by using one of the most powerful weapons against it, the one that will ultimately cause its demise; the one that will stop it in its tracks.

Communication!

Here are two examples of what I knew was possible.

A very Gentle Man, Mr. G shared a story with me; he was riding on a bus one day and a young lady approached him, she said "hi you don't remember me do you?" he said no. She explained to him that one evening while she was passing by him as he was closing the gate at his job, he spoke to her, "wishing her a good evening" and they talked for a while. She explained to him that on that day she was on her way to take her life, but that their talk changed her mind. A simple act of him being kind and gentle, as he is always, and allowing himself to be used by the Higher Power, in the way he is most comfortable. This natural occurrence, allowed for a life to be saved. By the way he works for the post office, he is not a practicing Psychiatrist, Psychologist, Social Worker or Mental Health professional. He is however, a Human Being, being the best that he could be.

The other example that I heard was during the course of being introduced to a business by B. Sharpe, I watched a video where the founder Mr. E was explaining his campaign to spread happiness. So, Mr. E's approach would be, "Hi may I have 30 seconds or your time?", is what he would ask you, then, "on a scale of 1–10 what level of happiness would you say your life is at?" When I first met Mr. E, in 2009, he asked me that question, my response was, "is 10 the highest"? Well in his journey Mr. E came across a young man who didn't have the time, 30 seconds, for the question. The young man responded with, "no and no again. Well long story short, they spoke for 30 minutes, after which the young man asked for his name and though Mr. E usually didn't give his name he gave it. Well the next day the young man called him, after researching Mr. E online and finding his number, and he told him that he was planning to commit suicide on the day they met and that Mr. E changed his life with their talk. To learn more about this happiness project visit: https://happyneighborhoodproject.com/37211.

WOW! Imagine how these two gentlemen must have felt, hearing these confessions, after the fact, thankfully.

What these examples teach us are two things; 1. We must know that our Creator will answer requests; you must keep yourself positioned to hear, see and feel the answers, and sometimes that means getting out of your own way and; 2. We can be valuable to each other, just doing what we naturally do, working with one another for the greater good and wellness of all. Realizing the payment for this type of work cannot be spent, and that you could never go broke of the joy that you will feel knowing that even without confessions, you have clearly have been a help to someone else.

There are probably so many stories that if told, would be similar to these. Some of us have no idea how we can have a positive effect on someone else's life. Be with positive purpose in all that you do.

You will find more information and stories on my website, as we receive them. In the meantime, make a positive, purposeful difference in someone's life, today and everyday, it will positively affect yours.

Please Read This Book With An Open Mind!
This book is not meant to be the end all solution or the one and only answer...

However, it is meant to be a part of the solution process, one more tool that will lead toward more lives being positively changed, for the betterment of all; it will also lead to reducing the number of lives loss because of suicide.

This book, short but to the point, should also help to open up a conversation about a subject that most people are "hush, hush" about...suicide.

There are many reasons leading people to commit suicide or have suicidal thoughts and not all of these reasons are from emotional disorders or present situations, as most people think.

Let's explore some of them "together", and work to put an end to them "together".

Please know that we all are powerful and full of gifts that have been given to us to use.

Know that once we realize our special reason for being, our lives can become fuller, richer and happier.

Before us, within our reach, is all that we need to fulfill the destiny that each one of us have been given.

Stay clear minded, keeping before you and around you, what and who helps to nourish your soul and your spirit,

All of which are where your strengths grow and your energy rejuvenates.

Evadynè

Let's Begin.....

Table of Contents

One

Profile of this Killer

This killer has no real relationship with its victims; however, there are commonalities among all of them. In these cases, the victims may have financial hardships, may have a personality that doesn't allow them to get along well or be understood by those they are surrounded around. There are some victims that have been abused verbally, physically, mentally, emotionally, academically or professionally, and others that may have physical, emotional or mental disabilities. Some of the victims have been victims of crimes such as social crimes against humanity, discrimination, humiliation, rape, bullying or could be a victim of a deaf ear, having no one who is really listening to them.

Suicide, this killer, takes its time and breaks down every single opportunity that it finds with its victims. There is so much power in words and so often people use words to harm others directly. This harm can also be an indirect action such as those speaking about you or on your behalf, who may not understand you at all. So, their perspective of you gets translated to another person, which can harm you by what they are saying. You sometimes have people speaking on your behalf to individuals who may be in the position to determine your resources and possibly your success.

People concern themselves with "curse words" as being abusive, and that's not always the case. Words of threat and fear can cause more harm than "curse words" ever could. Choosing your words wisely is so important.

This is why adults, who have a habit of speaking around children about their adult relationships, using words that are degrading and talking down about another person that the child may love and care about shouldn't do this. This talk can make the child have ill feelings about the person who is being put down and as children grow up with these conversations in their minds and feelings in their hearts, there begins an opening for this killer to enter. The child can't trust the speaker nor can they trust the one being spoken about, after the horrible stories that they have heard through their lives, so there is another opportunity for this killer to grow more and more.

The effect of this on the child, is no hope, no where to turn, no one to talk to...about the bully in school, about the sexual abuse, about the sex, drugs and alcohol being introduced. There is no "out" for this young potential victim....and here, in this hole of emptiness and pain, is where this killer finds an opportunity to plant itself and bloom...pop in and out like a Mexican jumping bean...in full sight of the inner soul of the victim. Now this person may still be a child or now a teen or have grown into an adult with underlying deep unresolved issues, and as life goes on this killer is in the lurks waiting for a weak time to attack.

This killer preys on people, who for a short time lose control of their thinking. Some victims begin to doubt themselves and those around them, which can leave an open door or window for the killer to creep in. Some victims engage in activities that alter their thinking, be it substances, organizational meetings, professional encounters or other entities not working in clear space in their own minds. These situations can allow weakness of thought and self-control and this killer is happy to find a new place to plant itself, patiently waiting to grow.

Once in, this killer imbeds into the thinking zone of the targeted victim, lying dormant, growing and waiting for the right time to strike. This killer, suicide, knows its victim's joys and is happy for their pains. This killer is sneaky. This killer is weak, that is why it never attacks when the victim is strong.

The most opportune time for this killer to strike is when all heck is breaking loose; loss of a spouse or mate, loss of a child, loss of a loved one of any form or faced with a repercussion of a voluntary or involuntary act and it is now full grown and knocking on your consciousness, asking to be let out, ready to play with all that it knows to be your weak spots. This killer has watched and listened to your deepest desires, because it has been there with a long time.

This killer is sneaky. This killer feels familiar, similar to the lyrics of music, themes of movies and video games, familiar and comfortable to you because it has become a part of you. Well shake it off...take control of your future; keep your happy thoughts near so that you can get to them quickly. Don't let this killer get the best of you. Now that you know how it looks, BEWARE.

If you are feeling that familiar feeling, that maybe this killer is lurking, know that this to shall pass and you will be okay. You may make a decision to change your life, but in a way that you will be able to appreciate and live through and live with, because you know how to live and enjoy life, right?

NOTE: All reported suicides are not a result of this killer. It is the reported cause of death, it is a copy cat, made to look like a suicide, and those are actually un-investigated homicides. They are accessory assisted, killings. How can you be under the care of true professionals and this killer become stronger? This copy cat assisted killer is the result of bad direction, medications and mind manipulation, which can be introduced by anyone

Therefore, when seeking care and someone professional to talk to...everyone should get a referral from someone they know and trust and get this referral before they are feeling down and ready for a change, that's when your mind is in a better place, when you are happy and can research and begin the process of keeping a clear mind and this killer out of your way.

What this killer does not want you to know are the options available. Seeking to visit a Psychologist, who does not prescribe medicine and who seeks to find the root of the problem, is preferable for some, over a

Psychiatrist who prescribes medicine that has many side effects, and lots of appointments. Investigate and compare the two professions and make the best choice for you.

If you are speaking with one of the professionals, insist that "you" can record the session, if they say no, then you may not want to use that person. Insist that they speak with family members, friends and co-workers as well, in recorded sessions, so that you can listen back on those conversations as well. Sometimes we are so removed from life, being involved in the doings and or preoccupied with life's issues that others see in us, and around us, what we miss.

Imagine feeling blue, down, in need of help, you go get the help and then the help tells you that there is no need to speak with anyone else in your circle; they tell you that your word, your version, is good enough. HUH? Sometimes those in your circle may have more details to fill in the blanks. Please know that your story is going to be your story, which is why you are there for help, but the question is, "how accurate is your story"?

Maybe speaking with a spiritual non-denominational Chaplain, Non-denominational because if you belong to and have been faithfully attending religious services, you have been guided by this faith and you may need a different angle to help you find your way back to a happier life. Grab a composition book with a pen, or a keyboard to type out your thoughts or a recorder to speak out your thoughts, and this can actually be on your cell phone device. Whichever method or methods you choose, listen or read what has come out of you.

It's very important to hear your story through your ears, so read it out loud, or have it read to you, it will resonate differently in your mind coming from the outside. When you are regularly thinking of something, over and over again in your mind, with the same abilities that you have, you will get a lot of the same results. When you write it out and read it or record it and listen back, those same thoughts will enter a different area of your brain; it then processes in that area, giving you a different perspective, in a different way. Try it.

15

The profile of suicide, this killer is this chapter; the accessories to killings will be discussed a little later.

Two

The Victims

The victims of this killer are of all ages. Young children and adolescents are among the rising numbers of victims of this killer. If you research this you will see that there is no specific race, age or gender that this killer will target and it obviously has a passport because it strikes worldwide. Adult professionals in all fields including healthcare, law enforcement and the military are among a growing number of victims. Teenagers who live in low sunlight areas, inner city communities and around the age of 13 are victims more often than we know.

Studies have shown that there is a direct relationship to the number of chromosomes in some victims which may have caused this killer to win. Odd that a popular baby formula laboratory was successfully sued, class action, for genetic testing over 25 years ago. Even odder, that they are still in the baby formula business today.

This killer lurks deep within so many people and there are many accessories to the demise if its victims. Victims have past experiences that are hardly remembered. Some are instances from infancy and some throughout their lives. These are experiences which can allow the killer to enter and find a place to grow.

We overlook so many situations that we are confronted with on a daily basis. We get upset, argue, drink, eat, smoke, and take risky actions all in the course of our lives. Never realizing that from these negative situations, deposits are being made in the soil in which this killer is growing; we are feeding it without knowing that it is there.

"Talk to someone", that's what is advised when one is facing depression, sadness, emotional illness, mental illness, drug abuse and other addictions. However, when you get to speak to someone, where do you start...from early childhood where sometimes bullying and abuse begins, on the playground, in school or at home or adolescence where a semi-freedom begins and choices start being introduced as exciting dares and the, "prove you are grown" challenges start arriving, or as an adult in an abusive relationship. Where do you begin, if you can't remember?

But again, who do you talk to about these incidents when they are happening? Now here you are a teenager or adult with a grown fully killer in your midst, imbedded deeply, ready and waiting to attack. This killer is offering an option that appears to be the answer to all the problems you are faced with.

This killer preys on the strong when they are at their weakest point; loss of loved ones, loss of income, loss of all hope and here it comes to the "rescue", but this is not the rescue, this killer is not the answer, this killer is not the answer, this killer is the weaker of all because at your strongest, it never shows up.

Then there are the victims of prescription drugs that cause suicidal thoughts, the ones we know about, the ones advertised. What about the combination of these medicines; what are the internal affects on the person's mind who's taking more than one medication, like three, four five, six or seven in a day? Are there studies on the combinations of drug interactions?

An example that I heard was about a Lady who is a dialysis patient, one day when she was driving her car, she heard, FASTER...FASTER...FASTER....NOW CRASH." She stopped the car. Thankfully she is a woman in her right mind, one that is capable of knowing right from wrong...and that the above idea was wrong. When she thought about this incident and what could have caused it, she looked into a new medication that she had been given and one of the side effects listed was "can cause suicidal thoughts". Don't we see that often enough on commercials?

The other victims of this killer are of greater numbers than the victims who passed on, we will call them Victims of Loves Lost, they are the loved ones left to wonder and remember their friends and family members. Left with so many questions of how this could have happened, why didn't they see it coming, why didn't the victim talk to them about how they were feeling?

So many valid questions, but let us keep in mind, we are not use to the language of this killer. This killer knows the victim so well that it hides the hurt and pain and it makes the victim look normal. Go to work, come home, play with the children, cook dinner, out with friends, everything is normal, doing their homework, locked in the bedroom, (as always), go out with no destination stated. Normal everyday life...how was your day...fine...anything new...no, okay love you...love you.

Well the Victims of Loves Lost are present today, to watch as this killer is executed, stopped in its tracks. Today they will have their say; together we will have a strong hand in stopping this killer. They will be victorious; we will all be victorious in this movement to end the trail of this killer with the lethal weapon, "communication".

Three

The Traps

Diagnosis of different illnesses; physical, mental or emotional have caused this killer to grow like a giant. People get the doomsday diagnosis, "nothing else we can do for you", well if not you, then who? Is what you should ask them and you should also ask, "Then what exactly, were you doing all along?" Now that we know a little more, we should ask these questions first. Ask about your options ahead of time.

Whatever you do, don't give up; get ready to fight for your life. Those spoken words are from one source. Go find another; Chinese medicine, naturopathic practitioners. Pick up a copy of the "Back to Eden" book, and actually you should seek these sources now, before you are sick, so that you don't get sick. *See Side Note at end of this chapter.

These are diagnosis, but as defined by who? What has caused these conditions? Most people who are diagnosed with depression are told that they are depressed based on symptoms described on television and radio commercials.

Ok, I feel sad, lonely and with no way out, but why is the real question and for how long have you been feeling that way? When did you or anyone in your circle begin to notice the change? These are very important questions that should be asked and the answers found in order to get to the root of the problem. Finding the root of the symptoms should be the start to the treatment process. When you treat the symptoms and not know the root, most of the time the treatment causes other symptoms and now the body is really confused.

The cancer family, the MS, the diabetes, the fibro family; what has caused all of these illnesses that can take you to the point of wanting to leave this life? You weren't born this way, so what has changed? Is it your diet, your environment, workplace or home? Is it in the air that you are breathing, sprayed perfumes, make-up, colognes, deodorant, your household cleaning products, your hair products and of course the foods you are eating?

This may sound strange but the chemicals being used to create these products are very dangerous to humans. This information is out there take a minute or two with your technology device, to research the product ingredients that you use and the protection garments used in the labs that create them. Our medical facilities will never on an ordinary basis, test you for these chemicals as the cause of your illnesses. If you work in those labs and exposure occurs, they would have specific methods to use at the hospital facility that you would be taken to and they are clearly directed on how to test and treat you.

Prescribed medications with several side effects are given to people who receive a diagnosis of depression. One of the side effects is, "can cause suicidal thoughts". To that we say, "Really, well thanks a lot". This killer has so many ways of getting into your system. Illnesses that can cause thoughts of sadness, loss, no desire to do anything and even suicide, are treated with medications that can cause the same or worse. In some cases, medications have caused these feelings, that didn't exist in you prior to taking them.

Other traps to consider would be street drugs and alcohol abuse which can alter your thinking and your decision-making skills can be altered. They can make you see things that aren't there, hear people that aren't present, spin around in the street, sleep all day and up all night. These elements can cause you to feel like the world is ending; and it just may be; however, you won't remember it when it happens.

These uses can cause you to make decisions that affect you and your family's safety. Then when you're back here with us, "wow...what happened?" you will be asking. You won't even know, or remember what happened, but thankfully you made it back, some people don't escape the killer so easily, sometimes the killer is the winner.

SSI Disability; there are some people who claim illnesses in order to receive SSI payments, which is making life financially comfortable for them, but guess what, if you aren't sick you will get sick from the treatments that you will receive and before you know it, you may be having this killer growing wild in your body, and it can be the side effects of all the medications interacting in your body. Your body can become a big ball of confusion.

Lyrics in some music will stimulate the growth of this killer. The songs actually promote and welcome this killer into the minds of people listening. The programs watched on all forms of media offer subliminal thoughts, suggestions into the minds and hearts of those watching. If these are bad messages, bad thoughts will come from them, and that's when an opening of the door will happen for the killer to attack, or enter for the first time, even when times are good, it finds a way in because it is all around us, at all ages.

STOP, STOP, STOP listening to and reading negative, "its normal" material. Because it's sold don't mean it's gold...for you. The term food for thought is so powerful when you think about it. We are what we eat, read, listen to and watch because everything goes into the brain. What goes in will have some type of an affect on our thinking, our dreams...it's designed for that. Know that, because it's funny don't make it good, because it's approved don't make it safe, for everyone. The traps allow this killer to sneak in and grow and the traps are all around us, but remember this killer is weak and will never ever win you over, when you are strong....so STAY STRONG.

Side Note...Check out bio-curcumin (turmeric), fiv-loxin (frankincense) and ginger, as anti-inflammatories, to fight inflammation which is what causes most diseases in our bodies. Pure green tea, whole star anise, sour sop, aged garlic and guinea root to kill cancer, and krill, SOD for brain health, Alcar with ALA, amino acids, probiotics, prebiotic foods, cruciferous veggies (broccoli, cauliflower, cabbage, brussel sprouts) just check out the nutritional value of your green veggies and all the others and fruits and foods. Check out "bananas" and their nutritional values for depression as well as turmeric. You will begin to feel a whole lot

22

better when you see clearer the value of natural remedies and begin to use them.

Visit the website www.NetworkingForSuccess.info and click on Invite Health for great products, and/or in your thank you gift, "Evadynè with Company...Talk Worth Listening Too", offers information sessions on cancer cures and health and wellness and so much more.

If you want to quit smoking, I have an idea: buy Nabisco gingersnaps cookies, (I know it has the high fructose corn syrup, which has mercury try using kelp and pristine chlorella which can remove radiation and toxic metals including mercury from your body) take a minute and break the cookie in 4 pieces, every time you want to have a smoke, put one piece in your mouth and just let it stay on your tongue, eventually swallowing it but more importantly taking in the flavor. You may need to start with a half cookie, depending on your desire, but try it. And if you are afraid of the weight gain when you quit, just start speeding up your metabolism, especially before eating. They say high aerobic exercise early in the morning will speed up your metabolism and burn calories for up to 12 hours.

There is so much that can be said for health and wellness, to keep people in a good place. There are Doctors who are advising amino acids for the brain to help fight depression, because our bodies are the greatest machines ever created, it too needs to be oiled and lubricated at times. Assessments of our basic needs for growth and development need to be checked, that would be a real physical check up. We need to top off and replace nutrients and minerals as our bodies may be unable to produce these naturally or have stopped the production process of necessary elements for us to run well.

There are some professionals who are really interested in helping the human body stay well, and they are doing their best to share that information. Actually, in the mid 90's, Dr Oz co-wrote a very important book titled "YOU, The Owners Manual", you can find it on his website, or mine. Why do we need, an owners manual? It's a guide to how we are put together and how we can stay together, for a long healthy life.

23

There is a Doctor that uses a special soup, garlic, ginger, white potato peel, celery, cabbage, white onion, cayenne pepper (all organic) to kill cancer cells, I would add turmeric and whole star anise for double power. There is so much information online. If you have a question, about health conditions, use your technology device and ask the questions. You will get several answers; ask for guidance from above to guide you to the correct one for you.

Use your technology device to learn something new everyday. Proven or approved or not, if it is not going to hurt you, give it a try. Be mindful that what is proven and approved is overseen by the medical business. Be mindful business always wants to stay in business. It is written "I have given you all that you need", believe it. We have naturally all that we need to be healthy, we only need to know how and the know where to get it.

If you are looking for a supplemental health plan to discount prices on most of your health care services including dental and a plan that's good for your entire household, visit:
https://24016872.savewithdiscounthealthcare.com or
https://24016964.savewithdiscounthealthcare.com
Also found in your thank you appreciation package.

Four

Botch Attempts

There are so many people who are ready to change their lives, end their lives, in the same way that suicide and suicide attempts will do. I call these events "botched attempts".

Here's the most common: knowing that you are sick and getting sicker and keeping it a secret. "Your private business" that you don't want anyone to know about because you don't want anyone to feel sorry for you. Well you should feel sorry for yourself, when you think about the fact that total strangers know about your condition (medical staff) but are not around to help you through it.

It also becomes a situation where your treatment providers are treating your symptoms and the possible oncoming conditions with what they know. They, however, really don't know other sources that can support you emotionally, physically and nutritionally, thereby creating a whole, holistic approach to your care. They know what they have been taught; but there's more.

So, what do you do, you keep it a secret, but at the same time you cannot spend quality time with family and friends so they start thinking that you are changing, lazy, angry and other characteristics that carrying your secret can cause. Then guess what, you begin to become sad, lonely, feeling like the world is ending, and because you didn't tell anyone your secret before, you find it even harder to tell them now.

What a problem this has caused to your healing and recovery. Support from friends, family and co-workers can uncover resources that may save your life. There are no secrets, so be the one to share your condition as soon as you know, so that your condition doesn't worsen.

Another is distractive living; driving, riding or talking while under the influence. Being in the way of any kind of traffic, walking, driving, or bike riding, while you are operating a cell phone, including taking selfies, this is very hazardous. People who knowingly ride with people who are under an influence are taking a chance with their lives as well.

Young people especially should not be drinking, however if you will be out with friends, select/designate a driver who will not be drinking or tired, to get you all home safely.

Then there are those who are so tired they can barely walk due to tiredness and exhaustion and they still take it upon themselves to drive. That normal quick blink of an eye, can take 3 seconds too many to reopen and there goes an accident, not only endangering the driver but also putting others in harms way.

This killer tries to pop in and take control of you, causing you to try little things to see if it works, like threatening others, in hopes of retaliation, trying new drinks or drugs because everyone else is doing it. These behaviors have a bad effect on your consciousness. When we know better but do wrong, this can have a very negative affect on the mind and body, allowing this killer a place to enter and lurk, in comfort, and it just waits until it finds the proper time to attack. There are no secrets, so when something is done that is wrong and you think that no one knows, well you know it and it can forever haunt you. Well these incidents can be true fertilizers for this killer to sprout.

Just don't do it! When you make a decision and your body, your tummy, reacts to it...it's the wrong decision. Think first, we all know right from wrong. So, ask yourself this, "How do I want to rest at night, with sleeping pills or a sleeping pillow?"

Five

Everything Happens In Its Time

We are here, on this earth, in this body for a period of time. What we choose to do with it is totally up to us. Well, once we are old enough or wise enough to make those decisions. Yes, our parents or adults have more control over our lives when we are young, however, to the young people I say; "change begins in the mind and planning the best future for yourself, in your mind, can begin the feelings of happiness today."

It's like, when you are having a fun school trip on Friday and it is only Monday and you are so excited that you can't wait until Friday comes. The anticipation and excitement of what your mind believes will be fun on that trip brings you happiness and joy all week. The same excitement can come with planning your future. Try it

Today may seem all gloom and doom, and other people's lives may appear more exciting; all is well and good; but tell yourself this, "as soon as I am able, I will do this and I will do that, and my life will take a different turn and I will be, look and feel happy always".

Everything happens in its time. Do know, that what we experience in our lives is about learning and lessons? Not always our lessons, however, we can still learn from them. You can call it sideways, hindsight, looking back and seeing what came out of it...what could have been done differently, how a different choice could have created a different result, and that's what living is about. What would make that experience better is if you would share the lesson with someone else, so quite possibly, if they were ever faced with it, they would have your story to rely upon.

27

There are no guarantees that everything will be perfect, but with perfect comes what? Perfect weather...well go out and play...perfect song...well dance until you are tired...perfect mate...enjoy everyday of it...perfect job, hooray...oh okay... but that is something to celebrate.

Everything happens in its time, just wait, be here, and the time will come that you will see why all things have happened the way they have. Listen to "Conversations with God" online. It is a bit revealing...it is food for thought....it may have some of the answers you are seeking, in a most inspiring way. Listen to it with friends, and then have a discussion about it.

Not everything we do, will give us the results we are hoping for immediately, but with the right plan in mind, and preparation, you will have a life that is rewarding and fulfilling. Keep steadfast in your thinking about what is best for you. Picture yourself there, in the plan, enjoying the scene that you set for your life.

Remember, it all begins in the mind, so that's why it is so important to feed your mind wisely, with your future in mind, having a long and happy life.

Six

Transformation....The Change

Who, what, where, when, why, how and are you sure?

Questions always lead to answers...and yes you can question and answer yourself. It is okay, in spite of what they tell us. Feed yourself with thoughts of pleasure, with ideas of greatness, read "right", listen "right", communicate and talk "right", keeping yourself in the company of goodness or no company at all.

When we are ready to make changes in our lives, not everyone will agree with the change, because they aren't ready. Keep in mind, even if you are a twin, "you" were born by yourself...given the strength and wisdom during that time that is specifically for you.

It is self evaluation time...who are you, who have you become, who did you think you were going to be, how and what do you feel has contributed to you being the way you are, seeing things the way you do? Did the music of your childhood affect who you are? The shows and movies you watched? The people who taught you? Can you remember the adults from your past? Were they kind and patient or angry and mean? Do you feel that any of these answers have affected your life and the way it is today?

How do you see yourself as you self evaluate? Now use others and ask them the questions above, ask them more questions. See who really knows you the way that you know you. This process will also allow you to see those that are not necessarily going to be with you in your new life. People we know for a long, long, time do not always know us best. They know us how they know us, based on how they view life, as in looking through rose-colored glasses. All things seem rosy, or maybe not. Well it works the same with people; how they view life is how they will see others and situations.

Like three people witnessing an accident and each one having a different story. This is based on how they view things, including how they see themselves. You can be looking at your life and this killer imbedded in you can cause haze to your view, so asking questions and self evaluating can help to clear the view in order to put your life together the way you want it to be.

Is this your time for change? Will others be affected? Absolutely. Will they live through it? Absolutely. For you to live the life you are headed to, you must realize that it is "your time". Your love for you, out powers the love you have for everyone else at this time, because if you are considering becoming a victim of this killer and letting it win, if ending your life, as all who know you, knows it to be...then your feelings are #1, you are the priority.

You don't need approval, you need preparation, you need to focus on what's next...what your options are...who do you want to be, where do you want to live...what climate is best for you...do you need a passport or a full tank of gas...do you need to learn a new language...or pretend you cannot speak at all...quiet is sometimes a blessing.

Put in your mind your new life...and the things you want to see, hear, feel, eat and touch. What is it that you want to see each day when you awaken in the morning...each night before you close your eyes? What are the sounds that you want to awaken to...birds...ocean...breeze...soft music....and when do you want to wake up and start your day...when the clock sounds or when your internal clock says, "okay now... stretch and arise".

Secret...ssshhhhh...when you awaken...lay for 10-20 minutes reviewing your night visits...your dream or dreams...see where they are leading you for the day...just lay. The same at night...when you lay in bed to sleep...let it be in quiet...just to review your day...your journey...let it pass as rest and sleep arrives...it's a very nice feeling.

30

Now, what's next...where do you go from here....and how will you get there?

There is more than one way to end life as you know it...just stay here and embrace the options before you. Now this decision may require you to live in a different part of the world or just in a different neighborhood; to associate with different people or no one at all, you know, to do some of your own thinking. Back to the basics again, the old fashioned who, what, where, when, why and how routine.

Look at your resources and see how far they can get you. What resources you ask? Well if you have life insurance, that isn't term, you have cash value or loan value in it, who better to use your money than you, who have been paying into it for years? If you have a pension plan or investments, you have access to funds either by cashing out or a loan.

Now those are some resources. If you own a home...consider taking an equity loan out, or refinance, rent it or sell it, provided there are no children in the home. Look at the ideal place you want to live and check out the purchasing, renting, sharing or exchange program that best suits you.

Note: If you need help with financial management, income taxes, life insurance, disability insurance, planning and investment strategies contact us and we can direct you to professionals that can help you.

It is **CHANGE TIME** and it doesn't mean quitting life altogether. **"Know That... You Are... An Example To... Someone Else"**

Pool your resources and see how far they will get you...not just away from your current world; that you no longer want to live in, but in the long run. Will your resources hold you for 6 months to 1 year financially? Should you seek a new job before you go? Register with temporary employment agencies, let your union know that you are relocating, find the stand-up comedy and open mic venues in the area that you want to live, because guess what, you may need to laugh or cry and also your story is one that will be a gift to someone else.

Do you like cruising? Apply to work with the cruise lines. Like flying?

31

Become a flight attendant or register for pilot school. It's never too late to start over, to start a new career. Find your passion and try to work in it. There is nothing more rewarding, and there is nothing you cannot get paid to do. Soul search inside yourself for your passion, for something new to do, that you will love doing everyday.

Look at what your professional life has been and see if you can make it a business. Market your services to the non-profit community and help others with the skills you have. Get help from people you know, to help establish your new career. There is so much power in people, and what we can offer each other, just for the asking.

Are you a professional and the pressure got you down? Go find work in a supermarket. Have you been unemployed for a period of time, can't find employment anywhere? Apply for public assistance or any government program and go through their work or training program or start looking for work again, because once you have a government program, you will get hired quicker because the company receives tax credits for hiring people who receive assistance. This includes unemployment.

Are you sick and tired of the symptoms of an illness that has you feeling down and out, a little hopeless? Well find another source of treatment with less pharmacy medications because some medications could be causing you to feel suicidal...it's a side effect of many medications and the combination of medications interacting with each other.

Again, keeping in mind that if you are feeling like this, the killer is lurking in your life, it is not necessarily your fault, and it could be caused by one of the accessories. Once you begin making changes, you may like your life; it may just need some life cleansing.

Try Chinese Herbal Doctors, acupuncture also Naturopathic Doctors plant-based vitamins and nutrient products, you can find some of the best information and product choices on my website, www.networkingforsuccess.info , Invite Health and others. Detox your body if you have the time. Cleansing the body helps to provide clarity of thought, and your decisions will become more focused.

Everything that we do should take some thought...but the question is, "what are you thinking with?" Is it bad energy, bad vibes, bad company? Are you thinking that this life is not for you...not your life? Well you may be right...so find it. Find the life that you know, to be the life you want to be living.

That's change in a way that you can live through and love yourself afterwards. It takes strength to make changes that you can walk ahead with. It's not always easy, but it is so worth it.
You will see....

Seven

Being Happy

Listen to the lyrics of the song Happy, by Pharrell Williams...do you feel that way? Can you feel that way? Like you're in a room without a roof...the sky is the limit...can bad news come along talking this and that and slide off you like wet spaghetti pouring out of a bowl? Can you see the sun through all of the clouds? The rain as a beautiful cleansing shower...to get started again with all the past washed away. Because life happens in ways we don't always understand... we just stay prepared for it and let it be and then be gone.

So how can you be happy? With all that's going on with you, with this world? Because happiness is within...it's about your life...the people you like...the things you like to do...to eat...the way you like to have fun...your music...your dance...think of the best place you have visited on vacation or would like to...and your favorite person at all ages, that you can remember...and the fact that you can still remember, that's something to be happy about in itself.

Those are many reasons to be happy...happy is within first...and no one can take that away. It's a wealth that can't be spent, but you can borrow from it, and borrow from others. If you know someone who always seems happy, genuinely happy...naturally happy, talk to them and asked the; who, what, where, when and why questions, about themselves.

Once you have this happiness, this inner joy and peace, you can never go broke of inner happiness or true happiness.

Can you relate to the lyrics of Just Fine by Mary J.? Feeling just fine...liking what you see when you look into the mirror...just pick a time when you had that feeling and keep that picture in your mind. Get back to it...to living in a happy space mentally...until you find that happy place physically, space wise, waking up and through your day with your "happy in mind". Keeping up the inside first and outside will follow...does that mean everything is perfect...NOPE.... just perfectly on its way to where you are "happy" all the time and everything is just fine.

Keep in mind that what you take in is what you will be made of. If you watch negativity, listen to negativity, read negativity then your life will be centered with that type of energy. When you have to walk that long block to the store, it's a long block, not the store at the end of the block. That is how you will be focused, the dreaded journey. Like the glass is half full or half empty; that's how you look at things. This thinking will determine how happy you see yourself being and what it will take to get you there.

If you understand this, and if you want to test it, start listening to, reading and watching more uplifting media, clean comedy, easy on the mind music, musicals, and love stories...find someone you enjoy hearing and listen to them on a device. Just try it...and let me know if things change for you.

In the case of adult relationships, it is not good to look for someone to make you happy. If you aren't happy within yourself, you aren't coming to the table with your half in place. If you look for others to bring you happiness, what will happen when they are no longer there? Well, there goes your happiness and your joy, and that's not the result you should be planning for.

Having someone add to your happiness and add to your joy is a wonderful experience, and they should be bringing their joy and happiness as well. If someone tells you, "I need you to make me happy"...RUN.

Who do you want to make happy? We want to make children happy, by exposing them to all that life has to offer them. Learning activities and fun things that brings them joy and lots of laughter. They need vacations and adventures to show them their choices. Senior Citizens and our

Parents because they deserve to see goodness in people after all their time invested and of course yourself. You want to be happy in all that you do, which in turn will shine on others.

Eight

Family and Friends Having Their Say

Sometimes they know us and sometimes they don't. Just because they were raised with you or grew up with you, does not always mean that they know you or how you are feeling and what you are going through. We keep a lot of things to ourselves and we should be speaking about them...even journalizing the things that are happening, because you get them out of your mind in that certain kind of way.

You can pretend that it is a friend that you are speaking about and this is the situation to get feedback without the person knowing it is you. Like having a bad day at work, with a co-worker who is odd; well sharing that information and the behavior of that person with a friend, may give you an idea of how to handle it, without getting yourself all worked up...at work.

When and if this killer stalks you and brings forth all the things going on in your life and invites you out of it...to take a leap...SAY NO, and GO AWAY. Call someone and talk things out. People can be judgmental at times, of others actions, and sometimes harshly, but just listen. Talk to 3 or 4 people throughout the week and hear what they have to say. Place in your basket what is good for you, the other stuff you can trash, it's like wrapping paper on a gift, sometimes you have to save the good and discard the bad or not useful. Remember because this is, "save a life time", there's no room for extra baggage. Remember this is the time that you will get feedback from several people that you know on how you are feeling, but as a suggestion, don't speak to all green people, find green, yellow, and gold people, and you listen to them carefully.

When and if you make this decision to change your life, there are some people that you may want to talk to. Your parents whatever their age, may not understand your decision, it is okay, you want to put it together in a way for them to receive it without criticizing them and you want to try to bring them to a place of comfort with the decision you have made, and why you have made it.

Some adults who are parents have not realized yet that we are all people, fair and even exchange of respect and appreciation is due. Some believe they are owed something for birthing and raising their children, and yes, they do deserve something, something like having a happy child, ultimately a happy adult, who was once a child.

That's the greatest gift of all, a happy child or adult after years of guidance and love. A child young or old, who is on the track of their success, not a track of escaping a controlled environment and taking whatever first offer comes along, but one who deliberately investigates their options, and make the best decision for themselves.

Your decision to change your life, as a living person may be hard for everyone, family and friends, but letting this killer make you a victim would be even harder. So go ahead and make your decisions, make your plans, set them forward and remember "when you decide and start living in your decision, your life gets better from that point on", even before you tell anyone, before you relocate, before you even make your first call. In your mind, your new life, your happiness has begun and that is where all greatness begins. Everyday will get better.

Having this communication session with your friends is also useful, because in all that you discover, you may discover that a simple misunderstanding was majorly misunderstood. That, what may have caused the tension, was a missed message, thanks to technology or a device completing your spelling sending the wrong message and no one questioning it. We must start communicating directly again or for some, start communicating period, verbally, or your direct source, which means not texting, so that you are understood correctly.

Please communicate if something really bad has happened, fault or no fault of yours, but you are liable, financially, please have that conversation with your spouse or family members, liquidate your resources to correct the problem or promise to correct it in the near future. But to let this killer, lead you to killing your family then yourself is so unacceptable. That idea alone shows the amount of love that you have for your family; that you don't want them to suffer for this error. Such a disheartening event, that so many lives will be impacted by, when there are other options.

Communication is the key...keep it open...keep it working...it works.

Nine

Don't Forget To Say Goodbye

Stopping this killer in its tracks and exterminating it out of your life. This chapter offers suggestions on how to say goodbye to the old and unwanted while moving forward in specific areas of your life as you build a new one; and you do have a right to build a new one.

The life that you want to leave behind has been handed to you, from your gender to your eye color to the city you live in and who you are in a relationship with. But guess what, now that you know more about yourself, you are entitled to create the world in which you want to live. This is with no disrespect to anyone that you love or who loves you, instead with a clearer and deeper respect and love for you and your life and the way you want to live it.

Now how do you start, knowing that saying goodbye to your old life isn't going to be easy? You first have to make the decision and then plan your change. Making the decision is 50% of the process. Mentally once you make the decision, you can begin living in it. Rehearsing how you will wake in the morning and the new things that you will do. The new way you will dress, the new foods you will eat, the new way you will wear your hair. All of these rehearsals are the beginning of being in a happier place.

Begin to plan your departure from your old life with all of the positive things you are working with. Don't worry if you find none, or very little, that could be the reason for your change from the existing life as you know it. Look at your options, your age, your income, your work experience, and your financial assets. Where will you live? Do you know someone who will accept you into their home? Do you have the resources to rent another place? Are you going to travel to another town, state or country? Remember in the beginning you didn't have all that you have and didn't know all that you know, so you are well armed to succeed.

This plan may take some time, time to save, time to identify the area that you want to live in, time is time but as long as you have it, use it, value it and make the best of it. Do you have to change your name? If so, can you remain on your same job with this name change, in the same school, can you recreate "you" in a way where you don't have to give up what you have created, choosing to keep the things you like or love in your life and setting aside the things that are not pleasing to you. This can mean family and friends, but with this killer loose, that just may happen anyway.

This plan is to stop this killer from taking you away from whom and what you love, and from taking them away from you. So go ahead talk to your friends and family, let them know how you feel about them, leave no doubt in their minds and give them a chance to speak, leaving no doubt in yours.

While saying goodbye, doesn't have to be so direct, it will give your friends and family an opportunity to know about you, the way you see yourself and also for you to evaluate your life through them, and how they see you, which may give light to how you are feeling in general, and if you are feeling bad about anything, ask the questions that you want answers to. This may be hard, however living in confusion and letting this killer grow inside of you is much harder.

All ages, know that this time will be the past, tomorrow, these experiences will be just that. Keep in mind that today is what matters. Stay in it, stay planning, stay making your changes and remember in your mind first will begin the feelings of happiness, and tomorrow will come.

Goodbye Old Life....Hello New Life...I am still here and will be here for a very long time.

41

Ten

Stop What You Are Thinking

If you are thinking of doing this just to make someone mad or make them pay for something they did you...you will never see their misery, if you are not here. Revenge is not worth your life.
Contact the National Suicide Prevention Lifeline
1–800–273-TALK (8255)
The deaf and hard of hearing can contact the
Lifeline via TTY at 1-800-799-4889
http://www.suicidepreventionlifeline.org/ GetHelp/LifelineChat.aspx
http://www.sprc.org/resources-programs/program-
encourageactive-
rewarding-lives-pearls
http://www.abpsi.org/find-psychologists/
OR KEEP READING

Please read this chapter with an open mind and a mind open...A mind that would consider the unknown as an option to what is known now. Guess what...you are worthy to you!

If this killer has made you feel less than worthy...know that you are bigger, better and stronger now, than you were 5 minutes ago. You feel this way, because you literally KNOW better of yourself. Therefore, you are worthy and valuable to you.... Now let's get your life back to where you want it to be... If you are thinking that you must leave this world today; that your life as you know it is not worth living and some others you know may agree with you, first, STOP talking to them IMMEDIATELY.

Now is the time to find your life, the one you want to live, not the one you want to leave behind. Start living a new one, make up your mind about what you want and let's go.

You made the decision, to leave all of this behind you. BUT YOU MUST REMAIN IN FRONT IN ORDER TO LEAVE IT BEHIND.

You must be willing to try something so extreme that others will be surprised. You may be the most surprised.

IF YOU ARE A CHILD OR TEENAGER:
Please know that these are times of hormonal changes, and these times are so under-discussed. Not only are you going through changes, but so are the adults in your life and no one is preparing you or them for these changes because many people don't understand them, don't recognize them and these changes show themselves differently in each person. Everyday and every change are different for everyone and many times unrealized even after the fact.

TO ALL:
Stay with us...this too shall pass, you have been around long enough to have seen that things change everyday. For better or worse they change, just stick in it and you will look back in a year and be able to talk about this time in your life.

Find your happy thoughts from anywhere in your life and hold them close, not as in I wish I was there again, but as in I was there, it was good and it can be good again, it will be good again with some changes.

Life is a revolving circle and around and around we go. Set your path for a better tomorrow and start right now. You need to get air, go outside and take in some deep breaths...take 2 or 3. Can't get out now, well open the window and let the breeze come in, even if its humid and hot...you are here to experience it.

You can go into the bathroom with some peppermint or lavender liquid soap (nice mix too) have neither, go to the kitchen and get cinnamon (use warm water for this) and put it in the tub and run the shower...let the cool water run to fill the tub while you sit on the floor and just inhale. Relax it gets better...always have and always will.

Listen to Adele's music she is therapeutic, each and every song. Go...set your path for a better tomorrow and start to take your breaks to relax and regroup, to gather your strength because this takes lots of strength and you have it. That is why this killer has never shown its face until now. There is something going on that has weakened your level of strength, just a little, but you are stronger than this killer will ever be. You are armed with tools not weapons to win this fight. These are tools that you have been using throughout your life; you just haven't had to use them in a long time, or in this same way.

Tell that killer...nooo, show that killer that it's your time to live your life in the way you know how to. Tell that killer that the execution day is today but not for you. Tell that killer that it has been stopped, exterminated, removed from your mind and body. It is gone!

Today is your day to begin your transformation, into a new life here on earth and nothing or no one will be in your way. You are getting back in the race, on the happy track, on the living track and moving right along into your life, the life you want to live.

Parents, who are reading this, please have a conversation with your children, no matter their age. Read this book together or apart and agree to have discussions about it. Write each other letters and give your views on it and share information with each other about what you need in your lives, to be happier. Write about the challenges that you are faced with and work on them together. Young people have the wisdom and knowledge of those who were here before them, before us they are meant to shed light on the lives of the adults they are around, because older adults have taught them.

44

Mind reading is a gift that all people have not received, therefore open communication is so important to getting life right. Sometimes we don't have a second chance, so take this one and do what you must do, for your life and those around you. Everyone has something to say...so be open to hear and listen.

Suicide is a killer and each and every person at the wrong time can become a victim. Execute this killer from the lives of you and your loved ones today. You cannot undo what was done or said, but you can acknowledge all that you know is possible and address it in the open. No fighting, no arguing, no placing blame. That's why writing out your feelings or recording them and listening together will allow everyone to know what's going on.

A LITTLE BIT OF TEARS NOW vs. A LIFETIME OF TEARS.

PARENTS PLEASE NOTE: As adults we are not in charge of our children's lives we are in charge of their well being. So it's important to know if their beings are well. That takes listening, not just hearing what they have to say and with no judgment. No placing blame and no redirecting blame. Some of the things that will be in the letters or conversations may be confidential, hurtful and a bit unbelievable. Be willing to believe what your child will say. If they need to be out of your home, accept that, it is what they need to be better. It is better to know that they are safe and that their beings are well, then to know they are unhappy and this killer is lurking in their souls, waiting to take it over.

BACK TO STARTING OVER...A NEW LIFE...STILL HERE....
Now this decision, as with many, may require you to make some serious and extreme changes. You may look to live in a different part of the world or just a different neighborhood, to associate with different people or no people at all to do some thinking. Going back to the basics again, you know... the old fashioned who, what, where, when, why and how routine.

Look at your resources and see how far they can get you. What resources you ask? Well again, if you have life insurance, that isn't term, you have cash value or loan value in it, who better to use your

45

money that you have been paying in to it for years, if not you? If you have a pension plan or investments, you have access to funds either by cashing out or a loan. If you own a home, then you may have the option to take an equity loan out, or refinance, rent it, or sell it, provided there are no children in the home. Look at the ideal place you want to live and check out the purchasing, renting, sharing or exchange program that best suits you.

It is **CHANGE TIME** and it doesn't mean quitting life time.

"Know That... You Are... An Example To... Someone Else"

Pool your resources and see how far they will get you...not just away from your current world; that you no longer want to live in, but in the long run. Will your resources hold you for 6 months to 1 year financially? Should you seek a new job before you go? Register with a temporary employment agency. Let your union know that you are relocating, see what help they can offer. Find the stand-up comedy and open mic venues in the area that you want to live...because guess what...your story is one that will be a gift to someone else and you yourself may need a laugh.

Do you like cruising? Apply to work with the cruise lines. Like flying? Become a flight attendant or register for pilot school. It's never too late to start over, to start a new career. Find your passion and try to work in it. Look at what your work life has been and see if you can make it a business. Market your services to the non-profit community and help others with the skills you have. Get help from the people you know to establish your new career. There is so much power in people, and what we have, to offer each other. Let's begin to use each other for the benefit of each other.

Are you a professional and the pressure got you down? Go find work in a local supermarket. Have you been unemployed for a period of time, can't find work anywhere? Apply for public assistance or any government program and go through their work program or training program for new skills or you can start looking for work again. In some countries, if a person is receiving government assistance, a company will get tax credits for hiring you. They will usually do what will benefit the company, first and foremost.

46

Are you sick and tired of the illness that has you feeling down and out, a little hopeless? Well find another source of treatment, with less pharmacy medications, which by the way, some medications could be causing you to feel suicidal. This killer has many accessories, such as the side effects of medications. Again, keep in mind it is not necessarily your fault, having these feelings of ending your life. Don't blame yourself.

Try Chinese Herbal Doctors, acupuncture also Naturopathic Doctors, plant-based vitamins and nutrient products, you can find some of the best information and on my website www.networkingforsuccess.info . Detox your body if you have the time. Cleansing the body helps to provide clarity of thought, and your decisions will become more focused.

Everything that we do will take thought, but the question is, "what are you thinking with?" Is it bad energy, bad vibes, bad company? Are you thinking that this life is not for you, not your life? Well you may be right, if so find it. Find the life that you know you should be living or want to be living. That's change, in a way that you can live through and love yourself afterwards. It takes strength to make changes that you can walk ahead with. It's not always easy, but it is so worth it. You will see....

Contact the National Suicide Prevention Lifeline
1–800–273-TALK (8255)
The deaf and hard of hearing can contact the
Lifeline via TTY at 1-800-799-4889
http://www.suicidepreventionlifeline.org/ GetHelp/LifelineChat.aspx
http://www.sprc.org/resources-programs/program-
encourageactive-
rewarding-lives-pearls
http://www.abpsi.org/find-psychologists

Chapter 11

Execution: The Art of Communication

The execution of suicide, this killer, will begin with the power of Communication on all levels until it is gone. We take it for granted, these occurrences, until there is another reported victim, or a victim close to us. Then we wish we would have done more, seen more or listened more.

Well get ready to be armed with more ways to keep this killer out of the way; and also keeping your family and friends prepared and armed to win. As often as the news airs, we will continue to fight this killer head on, until it is gone.

How do we communicate, let us count the ways...

Verbally
Speaking out loud, not loudly, about what is going on in your life. If you are being abused or if you are having feelings of being overwhelmed, being annoyed, being threatened, being bullied, tell someone, tell everyone that you are not feeling safe and secure in your space. Don't be afraid of sharing your life, the more you share, the more we all will learn; which in turn equals helping one another. If you keep this to yourself the attacker wins.

Not everyone that you speak with will understand what you may be going through, because again those rose-colored glasses, allows us to see in the way that our brain sees. You may be teaching someone something new, as you speak to them about your issue, so they may be surprised, which can have a positive effect on the situation you are facing, if their surprise causes them to begin asking questions; then there begins a conversation.

You do not have to be faced with something negative in order to have one these conversations, you could be sharing a happy occasion, a new recipe or dish you may have eaten, a new idea that you came up with or just happy to be in the day that you are in, and saying good morning, good evening or have a great day to the next person that you see. Someone said to me "you can have a conversation with anybody", I replied, "even a napkin, if it is clean".

If someone has come to you with an issue and it is heavy on your shoulders or your heart, share it with someone, but do not mention names without permission. If it is life threatening, then maybe an authority should get the report. We are all here for the greater good of the next person.

There is an art to listening; not just I am here, so I can't help but hear you. It is more like; I hear you and you have my attention, I am also listening to you. Listening requires attention; it requires you to be in the thought of the speaker, in an attempt to understand what they are saying and in some cases what they are not saying.

People at times, are so involved with themselves, that they only see and hear their point of views. Once they are telling the story to someone else, the story becomes clearer to the listener and the speaker. Hopefully, the listener will have an opportunity to ask a question or two. Those questions will expand the story and will help the speaker to realize a solution to the situation, or at least get closer to the solution, or a better end.

The Arts "Music: Drawing: Poetry: Singing: and Dancing"
Being artistically creative is a most wonderful gift of expression. It is an opportunity to bring out the inner you in a project; the feelings the visions, the freedoms, the sight beyond seeing, the joys, the pains, the melodies, and fame. Along with the pleasures that you feel when you see in others, the same expressions on their faces, the movements of their bodies and the tears in their eyes; the roar from their applause and

49

their exhaustion; the same as what you experienced in creating it, all of this is priceless.

There is much joy in using one of the art disciplines to create from within you. Keep in mind that even if you are not an accomplished artist, you can still do what each discipline requires you to do.

You can write out your feeling with words that rhyme or not. You can paint or draw a picture with what you feel and see inside and out. You can sing so off key, that if you wanted to, a studio can clean it up for marketing purposes (we have seen that done); but the singing itself is exhilarating, it is freedom of your expression. If you move a little, the feet, the arms, the head and shoulders even if you can't stand, because I have seen some mean chair dancing. All of these expressive techniques are done with no competition, no criticism, and no judgment. You and only you have to approve. All of these experiences can truly improve your life.

Movement of your body which is directed by your mind and guided by the higher power is extraordinary. Dancing, the watching of it and the doing of it is powerful. As in performances, you can get the story without words, feel the passion, the emotion without knowing the, who did it. Dancing is all around, no form or fashion, and sometimes no music. You are in it one way or another. Watch the movements of people walking on the street, you can see their movements as they dodge the cracks on the streets, the people passing them, the traffic as they crossover to the other side. Just watch. The movements of their bodies, it tells a whole lot about how the person is feeling and some of what they are thinking.

How we feel about life everyday is so important to what our future can hold. The ability to communicate through the arts is a tool that should be encouraged and continued through all aspects of your life.

Silence
When people are quiet it can be alarming, especially if they are withdrawn and quiet. Not just, I don't want to talk right now, but more like, I never want to talk. I never or hardly ever want to interact with the group. I shun away from engagements with people. I always sit by myself at lunch time and close my room or office door. They may be actually saying, "I may really need someone to talk to, because maybe

too many time outs as a child may have led me to feel comfortable in this lonely space".

If you see that type of behavior, it may be cause for alarm. Whether this is a child or an adult, the behavior should be watched. If they haven't been diagnosed with a disorder that would have these symptoms, this behavior may need some addressing. We get into habits that become normal for us, but not healthy. Being alone for to long, growing up an only child or oldest child with a long gap before the next sibling arrive, can cause this type of separation behavior.

But then sometimes, just sometimes, silence is good. It allows you to regroup, to refresh yourself. Know that because your mouth doesn't open does not mean that you aren't communicating. You may just need a station break, a vocal cleansing, a mind cleansing period, a "me" time, vacation. But please, if this is the case tell someone, a least one person so that if you aren't back within a certain time, someone knows when you left and where you went. You know?

American Sign Language
There is a community that, like many communities that aren't speaking the native language. I believe this community is so under served. How do we reach the hearing-impaired community, a condition that can affect anyone at anytime?

I suggest learning American Sign Language in order to have another form of communication, just in case you are unable to speak verbally or decide to stop speaking, and also this would be great as it will allow you to be able to communicate in most, not all, parts of the world.

Every public form of entertainment such as movies, plays, comedy shows, concerts and other organizational events should have ASL translators. The feeling of being included can improve the lives of many, making them happier.

Learn at least one new language, which ever one you choose, because communication is the real key to success at what ever you choose to do.

Cultural
There are so many different cultures living in the same country together.

51

Learning something about the different cultures will help us to understand why things are done a certain way, different than the way we are accustomed to. Have you ever asked yourself, why is it that when you speak to someone from another country, they look confused, not at you, but by what you have said to them? That's because words translate differently, from country to country, so, as they are looking confused, left eyebrow up in the air, like a triple dose of Botox, ask the question, "how did you understand what I just said"? Not that you are calling them stupid, but that they looked confused and if that wasn't your intention, then you want them to have clarity on what you said to them.

You should have a person's attention when you are speaking with them or to them; this is the main key to effective communication. You can walk into a room and say something and walk out under the belief that you were heard and understood. In actuality, you walked into a room where people were engaged in an activity. You did not get their attention. You said something and left the room. Well if what you said wasn't received, who would hold the blame if directions were not carried out? It is important to have the attention of a person when speaking to them. Knowing that we are understood, when we need to be understood.

Knowing that what you took your time to do or say; is being received in the way you want it to be. You having clarity of your thought; is one thing but knowing that your thoughts were received with the same clarity is another.

That can also be said and done in your own culture, with everyone that you speak to. To hear is one thing, to listen is something else. You should have people confirm what you said to them, not in your words that you said but what it meant to them when they received it. Especially when giving directions on something that needs to be done. This may seem childish, but it is the basis under which communication has been created. How much time would be wasted if all that is said and done is never received, in the way you want it to be received?

Body Language

Watching a person's body movements, is just as important as hearing what they say out of their mouths. Body language can be the tell all, to how you are feeling. Whether you are relaxed and comfortable or nervous and tense, your position of sitting, standing, how you walk, hold your arms or cross your legs. These positions can tell others a lot about you, without you saying a word.

When someone is speaking to you, do they have your attention, or is your head up in the air? Are you looking behind you, or are you playing with something in your hands, huffing and puffing like you can't wait until this talk thing is over?

Or, when someone is speaking to you, are you relaxed and focused on what they are saying? Are you hearing and listening to them carefully, taking mental notes just in case you have questions? Are you giving gestures indicating to them, that they have your attention, responding by smile or nod? These are good body positions for an attentive listener.

Communication is the key to success in all areas of life. Success isn't measured by money alone; it's also measured by the happiness and joy that is in your life and the lives of others you may influence. We must learn how to use all of the tools available to effectively communicate what is good and what is not so good in our lives.

The choices that we make daily can affect our lives today and in the future. Think long term when making decisions about the plan for your life. Be willing to modify your plan, not because of failure, but because we as humans are continuing to develop in our lives as we grow older and experience more. We are learning everyday something new, and that something can stimulate another thought, which can affect your initial plan. Now, what do you do? You re-assess your long-term plan and see how the "new" thing either fits in or what may be needed to change, to continue your plan for happiness.

As long as we are here in this life, on this earth, changes are going to happen. Stay prepared for changes. Watch the experiences of others and learn from them. Talk extensively to the older and wiser people in your life, or those you meet along the way. Talk to the children; ask their opinions on certain situations that you may be going through. Children are so knowledgeable and informative. We can learn so much from them if we just listen. Then when it is their turn to talk, we should do the same...listen.

Communication, It's Your Turn
"Suicide...Be Gone"

Note from the Author

Thank You Very Much For Reading This Book

I hope it that it will help you or someone you know to live a happier healthier life. When you make a decision that you need a change, it's not the end of your life, but the end of a life you have lived. There are so many ways to make changes. I hope you find a way through these pages.

Everyday is a new day, new beginnings, and new ideas. Using what you have learned along the way and getting to make different decisions about your life is a blessing. Someone always has more or less than any of us, but it's the joys we can find in what we have, and the happiness that we find in ourselves that allow us to be happy for others. Appreciating what they have acquired for themselves is good and we may see, if we like what they have, what we can do to get some of the same things.

Don't let this killer block your joy, and happiness, instead find your joy and your happiness inside. It is in there and if it is just one thing,
LET THAT ONE THING GROW TALLER THAN THE CLOUDS!

It is very important that we look at trends and customs and how they began. Once on a roll, people begin to believe, without question, that these behaviors and practices are "normal". There is a trend that causes suicide to be a hush, hush mysterious subject not to be discussed. Well if it's not discussed, as they discuss everything, anyway, then how will we ever be able to capture and conquer it? I was overhearing the lyrics of a song saying, "my friends are all dead, take me to the edge". I was like WHAT! It sounded to me like an invitation for death to come. That's so, unacceptable as it plants the killer into the minds of those listening, whether they know it or not.

There are people passing on because of suicide, who are successful, happy on the outside, have a luxury life from what we can see. They have all that they need in their reach. But something happens. What happens is the real question? What would lead them to want to end their lives?

People who are happy, living in a comfortable position, children who are happy and doing well in school, at home, with their friends and then they decide to end their lives. These instances make me think...hmmm...what could have gone wrong?

You have everything and more, you appear happy, your family is doing well. Sure, you may be using or have tested street drugs and alcohol on occasion which could be a factor, but who is helping you if these issues are a problem? Who are you talking to, if this killer is able to get the upper hand? What are they talking about? Who else are they speaking to about you? Is it anyone that you really know and who really knows you? What are they saying to them? Or are they reading from a manual, following other people's instructions? Being guided by the guidebook?

Then there are prescription drugs that cause suicidal thoughts. The ones we know about, the ones advertised. What about the combination of these medicines; what are the internal affects on the person mind who's taking more than one, like three, four, five, six or seven in a day? Are there studies on the combinations of drug interactions?

Again, an example that I heard was about a Lady who is a dialysis patient, one day when she was driving her car, she heard, FASTER.... FASTER.... FASTER.... NOW CRASH.... She stopped her care. Thankfully she is a woman in her right mind. A mind that is capable of knowing right from wrong. She knew that the above idea was wrong. When she thought about this incident and what could have caused it, she looked into a new medication that she had been given and one of the side effects listed was "can cause suicidal thoughts".

People are falling victim to suicide and their reason is because their friend or a loved one did the same thing. Well these victims have children, loved ones and if their thinking led them to follow their friend or loved one, would they would expect their children and loved ones to do the same?

Any kind of loss is painful however we see everyday that life goes on, not exactly the same of course, but for those who stay steadfast in it, it will go on. Let's start preparing young ones and older ones for the passing on process. Start having the conversation about, "when I am no longer here", or what do you want me to do when you pass on?

56

I use to call my Mother everyday, making sure she was awake, seeing how she was doing and then one day I asked her, "So Ma, what do you want me to do when you aren't here, when you pass on". She said "put me away in my red suit", well we met that halfway she was laid out in red and blue.

I was led to write this book because my view on leaving this life by means of suicide was, if you are ready, then okay. Not realizing that ready may not be your choice, it may be the accessories, including prescription and non-prescription drugs. I did not agree with departing without conversation with loved ones. I didn't feel that it was fair to leave such an empty hole full of questions. Then I had two conversations, thank you Dr. B. for the look you gave me, that made me think, and after a couple of days of thinking, I realized that leaving this life does not mean by way of death.

Change, transformation and shifting gears, those are better moves, better experiences, having an actual adventure, imagine that. I know there are people who won't agree with the change or transformation process, but that would be out of selfishness. Love for the person who is changing should outweigh selfishness; one should hear the need of the person who desires the change.

"Till death us do part", pretty strong words. I and others take words seriously, so I don't say those. I don't encourage people to say them, for these same reasons; 1. Because life is to long, as it should be, and development continues and sometimes people continue to grow and grow apart, not the love but the interests and their long term plan and 2. The harsh act of murder/suicide. That closeness and commitment is one that can be held tightly, with the "till death us do part" statement. Love someone enough to want their happiness as much as yours, in spite of the inconvenience it may cause. If this killer gets its way that would be inconvenience, confusion and a great loss.

I wanted to give an understanding of suicide from my perspective and help to put an end to its force on people of all ages. It's happening too often and more often than we know. Something has to be done. We must build an awareness of this killer; demystify it, so that people aren't afraid to talk about it, beyond the medications to manage the thoughts of it and the commercials and the news after the fact.

People feel that it is a touchy subject; that it may be too close for someone to discuss. Why is it touchy? Taboo? The "do not talk about it subject? Maybe because it leaves such a big "empty" hole that is full of questions, that no one can answer. Finding possible sources of how it can begin and with early detection, open communication and eliminating tools together we can nip this thing in the bud as they use to say. One step at a time, which is the goal.

I remember hearing news reports about parents killing their children and saying there was too much pressure. Family members and friends in shock, of course and saying, "They should have said something; I would have taken the children". So now if that should happen in the future, someone comes to you and say they are overwhelmed and need a break, don't judge them, instead, HEAR, LISTEN and UNDERSTAND their cry. If you can't take the children find someone "now" who can, just in case you get that call.

If your child or teenager is going through something like the puberty process, a hormonal crisis, keep an eye on them even before that expected age, (which we don't know when that is now) watch and understand that they know not what they are doing. Neither did we during that time. We can all remember the "when I was your age stories". Each generation arrives with more than the previous. Remember the when I was your age my mother would have done xyz...know that their parents your grand parents, heard and said the same to them.

Some signs of change in children are obvious. We see the outward, hair growth, voice cracking, cycles starting, breasts developing, but what aren't we seeing? We aren't seeing the force of "grown" shooting through their veins giving them the ability to reason and understand in an adult way. We don't see the feelings that they feel when they are being spoken down to, like we are speaking to a young child while inside they are changing into young adults. These awkward feelings can cause rebellious behavior and here is an opening for confusion and

anger which this killer will find a place of entry to plant and grow and that's not what we want. We must be observant and stay awake to all the possibilities that are out there. With technology constantly in our hands, get three versions of hormonal changes and what internally it affects. Also research the other elements that are out there and affecting our children, our future.

Be easy and patient with people in your life, people who you encounter, especially young people and senior citizens (my two favorite groups). The two groups who know little and those who know they knew more. There are so many elements that can come into the lives of people at all ages. Be prepared and don't get caught off guard. Know that changes are not expected all of the time and the reaction to the changes can really be frightening. These changes can cause people to be defensive, or on guard so be careful because the punch may come your way...unexpectedly.

While we have time, let us become an inspiration to ourselves first, then to others. Be careful what you say to people, because once it is said it cannot be taken back. I am sorry, does not erase if from the mind. I apologize, well that either. Also remember apologizing means that you will not intentionally do it again. Say it and mean it. Actually...whatever it is that you say, you should mean. Thinking before speaking is a very good practice to put in place and a good practice to keep in place. Also sharing that information with children may be a good idea. I am just making a suggestion.

If you have lost a loved one in any way, please know that there are people who can help you. To leave a comment, review this book, join in on a conversation, or to read the comments visit: www.NetworkingForSuccess.info or call 347-457-2769.

Best Of Life To You All,

Evadynè

As a special thank you, we offer you an appreciation package; the Networking For Success Access Power Portal.
www.NetworkingForSuccess.info/Power_Card_Network.html

©August 22, 2017
ISBN-13:978-1983667237
ISBN-10:1983667234

The following blank pages are for the reader to make notes. I know how important it is to catch thoughts when they come, so this space is just in case.

More Notes:

More Notes:

More Notes:

More Notes:

More Notes:

More Notes:

More Notes:

More Notes:

More Notes:

More Notes:

More Notes:

Thank You!

Made in the USA
Columbia, SC
21 September 2018